Contents

KU-053-213

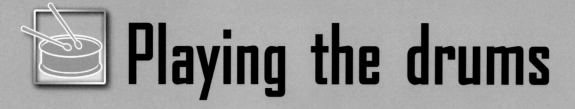

Playing the drums

Playing the drums is one of the most energetic and exciting musical pastimes. Drummers are essential to music that has a beat, as they help provide **rhythm** and make sure that the rest of the band play in time together.

Who can play?

Anyone can learn to play the drum kit, but you do need to have a basic sense of rhythm. With time and practice, the coordination between your hands and feet will improve and you will be able to play different rhythms at the same time on different parts of the drum kit. The positions described in this book are for right-handed players – you will need to reverse them if you are left-handed.

Drumming technique requires a lot of coordination, as you will be using both hands and both feet at the same time.

Drumming

Ian Adams

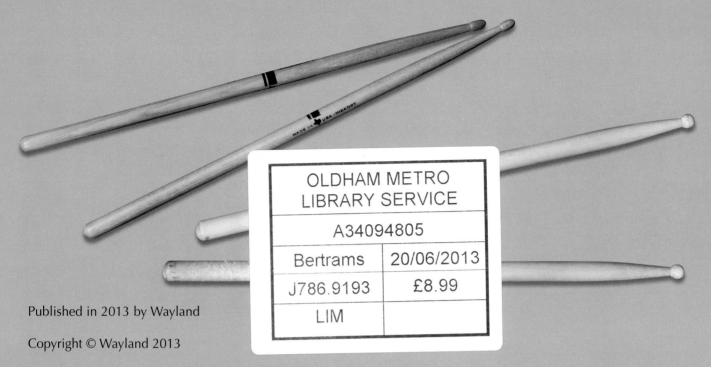

Published in 2013 by Wayland

Copyright © Wayland 2013

Hachette Children's Books
338 Euston Road
London NW1 3BH

Wayland Australia
Level 17/207 Kent Street
Sydney NSW 2000

Series editor: Rasha Elsaeed
Editor: Julia Adams

Produced by Tall Tree Ltd
Editor, Tall Tree: Neil Kelly
Designer: Jonathan Vipond

British Library Cataloguing in Publication Data
Adams, Ian.
   Drumming. -- (Master this!)
   1. Drum--Methods--Juvenile. 2. Drum--Instruction and study--Juvenile.
   I. Title II. Series
   786.9'193-dc22

   ISBN: 978 07502 7191 2

Printed in China

Wayland is a division of Hachette Children's Books,
an Hachette UK company.
www.hachette.co.uk

Picture credits
All photographs taken by Michael Wicks, except;
t-top, b-bottom, l-left, r-right, c-centre
1 and 5 Dreamstime.com/Kathy Wynn, 7br Dreamstime.com/Klotz, 17tl Mandy Hall, 18 Istockphoto.com/Alan Crawford, 23t Dreamstime.com/Dreamcatcherdk, 24cl Dreamstime.com/Vangelis, 25tr Magnus Manske, 25cl Diego DeNicola, 26cl Dreamstime.com/Sherri Camp, 27tr Craig Lovell/CORBIS, 27bl Dreamstime.com/Kristina Afanasyeva, 29t istockphoto.com, 29br istockphoto.com/Gremlin

The website addresses (URLs) included in this book were valid at the time of going to press. However, because of the nature of the Internet, it is possible that some addresses may have changed, or sites may have changed or closed down since publication. While the author and publisher regret any inconvenience this may cause the readers, no responsibility for any such changes can be accepted by either the author or the publisher.

Disclaimer
In preparation of this book, all due care has been exercised with regard to the advice, activities and techniques depicted. The publishers regret that they can accept no liability for any loss or injury sustained. When learning a new activity, it is important to get expert tuition and to follow a manufacturer's instructions.

Acknowledgements
The publishers would like to thank Yanna Marie Avlianos and Joe Bamford for their help with this book.

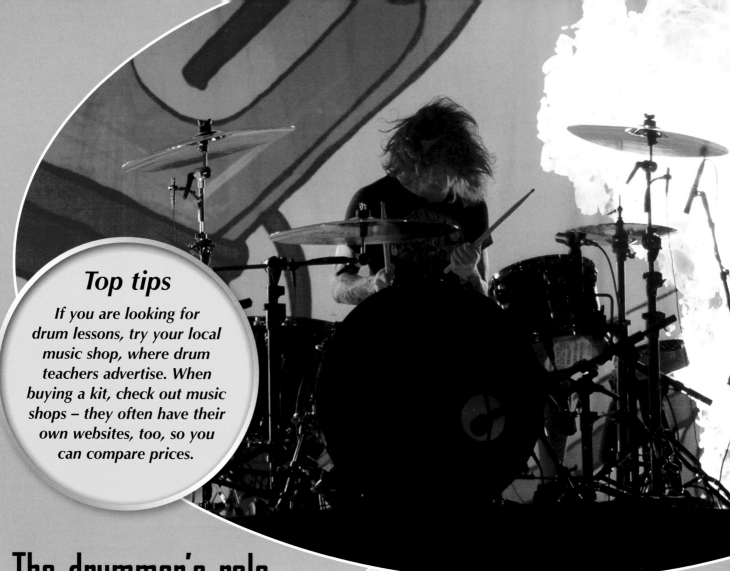

Top tips

If you are looking for drum lessons, try your local music shop, where drum teachers advertise. When buying a kit, check out music shops – they often have their own websites, too, so you can compare prices.

The drummer's role

The person sitting behind the drum kit is an important part of a band. The drummer is responsible for counting the band in to start a piece of music and, once the band has started, the drummer has to keep a strict rhythm so that everyone plays together. If the drummer speeds up, so will the rest of the band, and if the drummer slows down, the band will follow as well. Keeping the right tempo, or pace, is far more important than being able to play a flashy drum **solo**.

At live rock concerts, the drummer sometimes gets a chance to show off and play solos. These are often accompanied by stage pyrotechnics – bangs, flashes and shooting flames.

Getting physical

Playing the drums can be physically demanding. Drumming for 90 minutes requires a good level of physical fitness – a drummer can burn up energy and experience a rise in heart rate to the same level as a professional athlete.

Types of drum kit

There are two types of drum kit used in popular music: acoustic and electronic. **Acoustic drums** do not need any form of amplification for them to be heard, while electronic drums need an amplifier.

Choosing your kit

When deciding whether to use an acoustic drum kit or an electronic one, it is important to think about volume. An acoustic kit does not have a volume control, and your neighbours will not be happy if you start playing it in a flat. If noise levels are an issue, then an electronic drum kit would be best. However, electronic drum kits can cost twice as much as acoustic drum kits.

Crash cymbal

Middle tom

Low tom

Types of cymbal

Cymbals are circular pieces of metal, mounted on stands, that come in different sizes. There are two hi-hat cymbals that are operated by a foot pedal, **ride cymbals**, which are used to play a steady rhythmic pattern, and **crash cymbals**, which are used to provide accented notes.

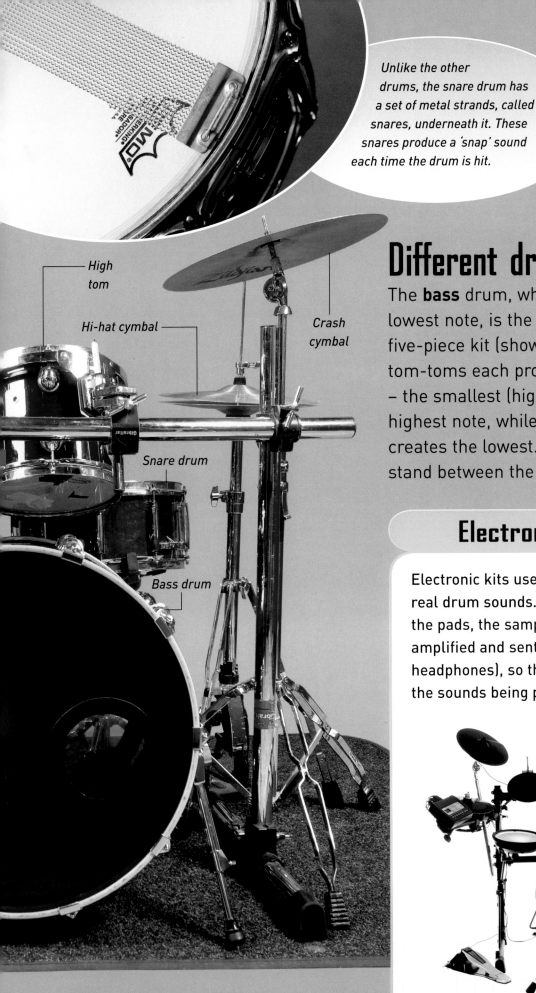

Unlike the other drums, the snare drum has a set of metal strands, called snares, underneath it. These snares produce a 'snap' sound each time the drum is hit.

High tom

Hi-hat cymbal

Crash cymbal

Snare drum

Bass drum

Different drums

The **bass** drum, which produces the lowest note, is the largest drum in a five-piece kit (shown left). The three tom-toms each produce a different note – the smallest (high tom) produces the highest note, while the largest (low tom) creates the lowest. The snare sits on a stand between the drummer's knees.

Electronic drums

Electronic kits use digital **samples** of real drum sounds. When a drummer hits the pads, the samples are triggered, amplified and sent to a loudspeaker (or headphones), so the drummer can hear the sounds being played.

Drumming equipment

To play your drum kit and to help you practise, you will need a few essential pieces of equipment. These will allow you to hit the drums, sit properly at the kit, keep in time and even protect your hearing.

Sticks and stools

Sitting with good posture will help to prevent tiredness and damage to your back. An adjustable, padded seat is a good investment. Avoid a stool with a backrest as it will encourage you to slouch. Drumsticks come in various sizes and lengths, and are made from wood. Some sticks have plastic tips to make the cymbals sound louder. Some drummers use special **brushes** to create a quieter rhythm.

Drumsticks are tapered, with the shaft narrowing at the top into a thinner 'shoulder'. The drum is usually struck with the rounded tip, or bead.

The drum stool, or throne as it is called, is a three- or four-legged padded seat that can be adjusted to suit your height.

Top tip

Drum stools are available in several shapes and sizes – some are round, while others are rectangular or shaped like a saddle. Try out a few different types of stool to find the one that best suits your height and build.

Earplugs (left) help to protect a drummer's hearing when playing for long periods of time. Drum machines (above) enable you to program rhythms in many musical styles.

Rhythm and volume

A **metronome** or drum machine is a device that delivers a steady beat. It will help you to play rhythms in time and at different speeds. If you play an electronic drum kit, you will need headphones or an amplifier, or amp. An amp receives electrical signals from the drum kit and changes them into the sounds that you hear through a loudspeaker.

Headphones

A 50-watt amplifier is a reasonably loud amp which can be used to practise and perform. Invest in good quality leads to carry the signals from your kit to the amp.

Setting up

The bass drum pedal should be attached firmly to the middle of the rim at the bottom of the drum.

When setting up your kit, make sure you can reach the drums and cymbals easily. The less distance there is between parts of the kit, the easier it is to stay in time.

Getting started

The bass drum is the first piece of the drum kit to position. It is placed on a rubber mat or a piece of carpet to stop it from creeping forwards while it is being played. Put a large pillow or blanket inside the bass drum so that it does not play too loudly and produce rattling sounds.

Positioning the tom-toms

Position the tom-toms around and above the bass drum. The highest pitched tom-tom should be on your left.

Set up the rest of the tom-toms from left to right as shown above. If you have a floor tom, it should sit on the floor to your right.

Mounting cymbals

The crash and ride cymbals sit around and above the tom-toms. Mounted on top of their own stands, they are held in place by wing nuts and pieces of felt. The stand-mounted hi-hat sits to your left so that you can operate the hi-hat pedal with your left foot.

The snare drum sits on its own stand between the drummer and the bass drum.

Crash and ride cymbals

A crash cymbal is mounted on its stand through a hole in the centre of the cymbal.

The crash cymbals should be set up either side of the kit, with the ride on the right.

Setting up the hi-hat

The bottom hi-hat cymbal is placed onto its stand with a piece of felt above it.

The top hi-hat cymbal is then inserted above the bottom hi-hat cymbal.

Sitting and gripping

Before you start to play your drum kit, you will need to learn how to sit correctly and how to hold the drumsticks, so that they are easy to play.

Good posture

Playing the drums with a good posture is very important. Sitting with a bad posture can damage your back and make you tire quickly. The seat should be in a central position. When your feet are on the bass and hi-hat pedals, the knees should be bent a little more than 90 degrees.

Good posture will see your back straight and your thighs angled slightly downwards towards the bass drum.

Sitting basics

Poor posture will see your back slouched and your legs bent too much.

If your stool is not at the correct height, adjust it by spinning the seat.

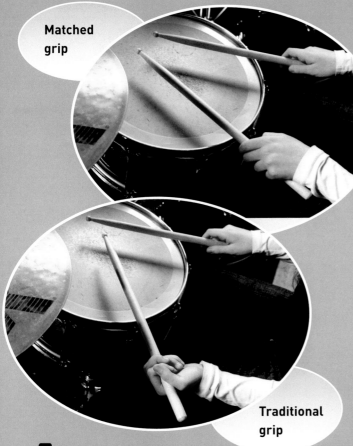

Matched grip

Traditional grip

Get a grip

The main types of grip are the matched grip and the traditional grip. Today, most drummers use the matched grip, where both hands hold the drumsticks in the same way. The traditional grip sees the left hand hold the drumstick at a slight angle with the palm facing up. It developed from playing a drum while marching. Using the traditional grip can make it difficult to play loudly for modern music styles, such as rock. It is more suited to older styles, including jazz and blues. Try out each style to see which suits you.

The fulcrum

The **fulcrum** is the point at the top joint of the index finger. The drumstick should be gripped between the thumb and the fulcrum, with the rest of the fingers holding the stick lightly so that it can bounce and pivot from the fulcrum. Try to have 2.5 cm (1 inch) of the bottom of the drumstick sticking out from the base of your hand.

The drumstick is gripped between the thumb and forefinger.

The other fingers wrap around the stick lightly but firmly.

Top tip

Top drummers make playing look easy because they remember that 'it is all in the wrists'. Keeping your palms facing towards the kit will help you to develop more control and good technique.

Theory and rhythm

Drummers can keep a record of their rhythms by writing them down. To do this they use a system of lines and dots called musical notation.

Writing rhythms

Rhythm is any regularly repeating pattern of beats. These beats are written down as a series of dots (called notes) that sit on a group of lines, called a stave. The type of dot used shows how long each note is, such as a quarter note (**crotchet**), eighth note (**quaver**) or sixteenth note (**semiquaver**).

Learning to read drum notation enables you to play other drummers' rhythms.

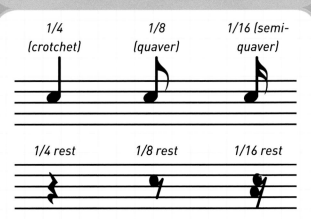

Musical notation

1/4 (crotchet)	1/8 (quaver)	1/16 (semi-quaver)

1/4 rest	1/8 rest	1/16 rest

Note length is based around subdivisions and multiples of a 'whole note', also called a **semibreve**. The length of a quarter note, or crotchet, is equivalent to one-quarter of the duration of a whole note. An eighth note is one-eighth of the length of a whole note, and so on. A dot after a note adds on half the note's time value, so a dotted quarter note is equal to a quarter note plus an eighth note. Symbols called **rests** are used to indicate periods when you should not play.

Time signatures

Musical notation is usually broken up into regular sections called bars, and one bar is separated from another using a vertical line called a bar line. At the start of each stave is a pair of numbers called a **time signature**. The top number tells you how many notes there are in each bar, while the bottom number tells you the type of note. **Repeat symbols** show whether a drummer has to repeat a bar, a few bars or a whole section.

15

Bar basics

The 4/4 time signature indicates four quarter notes in each bar; 6/8 signifies that there are six eighth notes per bar. The dots at both ends show that the section must be repeated.

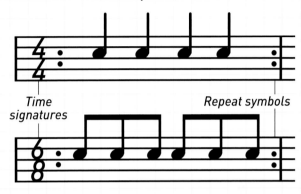

Time signatures

Repeat symbols

Drum symbols

A drum **score** (musical notation showing drum parts) is made up of the notes, the stave and the time signature. The dots on the five-line stave do not just show the length of the notes – they represent the parts of the drum kit. Using these special symbols, the full range of drum rhythms can be written down. Each piece of the drum kit is shown on a different line on the stave, or the space between two lines. The most commonly used symbols are shown below.

Crash cymbal

Hi-hat (open, played with stick)

Ride cymbal

Middle tom

Snare drum

Bass drum

>

Low/floor tom

Accented snare ('>' indicates **accent**)

High tom

Hi-hat (closed, played with stick)

Hi-hat (closed, played with foot pedal)

15

Building up rhythms

You can put various notes together to create a rhythm, or groove. Each groove is built up from various repeated sets of notes. Each repeating set is called an ostinato.

Starting off

Creating a groove requires coordination between your hands and feet. A simple pattern combining the hi-hat cymbals (using your right hand), the bass drum (right foot) and the snare (left hand) is a good place to start building up your drumming abilities.

Top tip

It is very important to count out loud when you first start to create grooves. This will help you to keep control of your timing, while your hands and feet play different rhythms.

Playing a groove

Begin by starting an ostinato on the closed hi-hat, playing repeating groups of four eighth notes. Try playing the bass drum and hi-hat together, then try the hi-hat and snare drum.

Build up the constant eighth-note rhythm pattern on the closed hi-hat.

Now play the bass drum on the first and third beat of each group (score 1).

Play the snare instead of the bass drum, but target the second and fourth beat (score 2).

Star file

CINDY BLACKMAN
Jazz and rock virtuoso

Cindy Blackman rose to fame playing with rock guitarist Lenny Kravitz. She now plays her first musical love, jazz, and has recorded numerous albums under her own name.

Putting it together

Once you can play scores 1 and 2 (below), try to put them together. Play the bass drum on beats one and three, the snare drum on beats two and four and the hi-hat on all eight beats (score 3). This groove forms the basis of many rock and pop songs You can then vary the rhythm of each bar to create a two-bar phrase (score 4).

Drum rhythm scores

Beats: 1   +   2   +   3   +   4   +

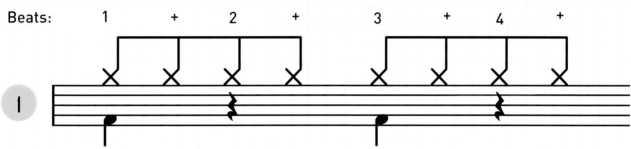

1 The hi-hat plays constant eighth notes and the bass drum joins in on beats one and three.

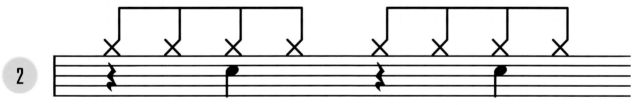

2 The snare drum replaces the bass drum, playing quarter notes on beats two and four.

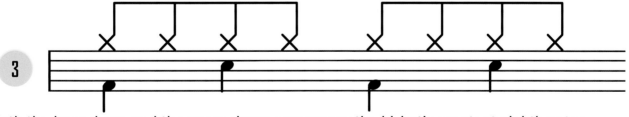

3 Both the bass drum and the snare drum accompany the hi-hat's constant eighth notes.

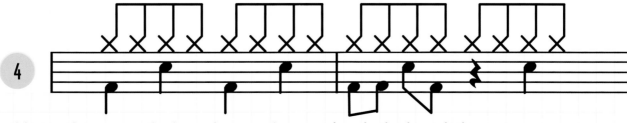

4 In this two-bar score, the bass drum and snare play rhythmic variations.

Drumming rudiments

Rudiments are the building blocks for drumming. They are patterns that can be put together to create drum fills and grooves. They were developed during warfare to communicate orders above the noise of the battlefield, but have now been applied to the modern drum kit.

Basic rudiments

There are 26 standard rudiments (although several more have been added), each with a specific name and pattern of beats. These include rolls, paradiddles and double paradiddles (see box, right). Rudiments are also used by drummers as practice exercises because they help to develop strength, control and coordination between both hands.

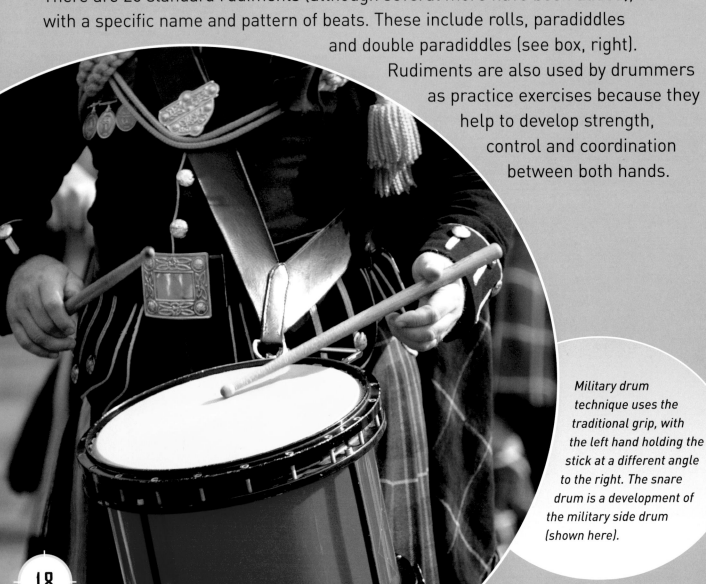

Military drum technique uses the traditional grip, with the left hand holding the stick at a different angle to the right. The snare drum is a development of the military side drum (shown here).

Three types of rudiment

A roll is a continuous sound created using a series of strokes. Rolls can be played with alternating (left and right hand) single strokes or multiple strokes of each stick.

Single roll The rudiment above shows a basic roll using alternating single strokes.

Paradiddle A group of eighth notes made up of a mixture of single and double strokes. The 'para' describes the rhythm of the alternating single strokes and the 'diddle' the double strokes.

Double paradiddle This the same as the paradiddle, but with two extra single strokes at the start. To describe this rhythm, we say 'paraparadiddle'.

Only the stick playing the accent comes away from the drum. Keep the other stick close to the drum.

Introducing accents

Accents are used to make certain notes louder than others, giving those notes greater emphasis. In a bar of four quarter notes, start by putting accents on beats one and three (the down beats). When you are comfortable with these, try the accents on beats two and four (the in-between up-beats). You will notice how this adds energy to your groove.

Coordination basics

To develop your drumming skills, you will need to work on your coordination. There are many exercises that will help to improve the way your hands and feet operate in unison (together) and independently.

Adding sixteenths

When you are comfortable playing eighth notes, you can play quicker sixteenth notes. To help you with the rhythm, you can count out loud, but instead of counting up to 16, you can count each group of four notes, saying '1 e+a, 2 e+a,...' and so on, which is easier to say against the quicker sixteenth notes.

By practising your rhythms, your drumming will become more relaxed and confident. This will allow you to add feeling to the groove.

Practising rhythm patterns

Musical notes can be divided up into many different types of smaller note. These are called sub-divisions. Practising sub-divisions with the help of a metronome will improve your ability to go from playing slow beats to faster beats in a more controlled and smoother way. The scores here show quarter notes, eighth notes, eighth-note triplets and sixteenth notes. Triplets are groups of three notes played in the same time as two notes.

Count '1 2 3 4' for simple quarter notes. Practise these on the snare drum, as shown.

For eighth notes, count '1 + 2 + 3 + 4' (see page 17 for eighth-note grooves).

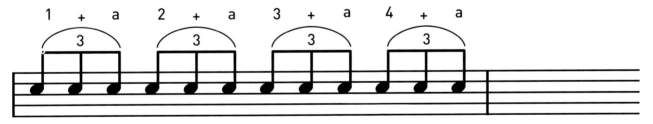

When playing eighth-note triplets, count '1 +a, 2 +a, 3 +a, 4 +a'.

For sixteenth-note rhythms, count '1 e+a, 2 e+a, 3 e+a, 4 e+a'.

Top techniques

The techniques shown here will take some time to get right, but mastering them will let you play songs in many different styles.

Dotted rhythms

To make grooves more varied and exciting, drum rhythms often use a mixture of note lengths. Sometimes grooves feature dotted notes – a dot after the note adds on half the note's time value (see page 14).

Rests are also used to add interest. These musical pauses break up the groove, enabling different parts of the drum kit to drop in and out of the rhythm.

Top tip

Listen to the drum parts in many different styles of music. This will make you more creative and give you an awareness of how to approach these styles in a live musical situation.

New rhythms

These grooves include quarter notes, dotted eighth notes, sixteenth notes and rests.

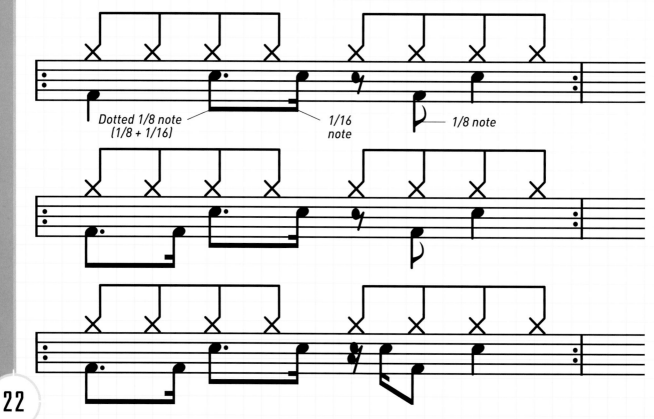

Dotted 1/8 note (1/8 + 1/16)

1/16 note

1/8 note

In the rock band Toto, drummer Simon Phillips expands his range of sounds by using two bass drums.

Double bass

Some types of music require two bass drum parts. Instead of having two expensive bass drums to carry around, however, you can simply add another pedal to a single bass drum. Two bass drum parts are usually associated with heavy metal, but they are also used in rock and jazz styles.

On the bounce

When you play a stroke with a drumstick, the stick will bounce away from the drum, if you are holding the stick correctly (see page 13). This bounce can help you play multiple strokes with one hand, but it needs to be controlled to save energy for the next beat.

If you are not careful, the drumstick will bounce away from the snare.

Keeping the drumsticks close to the snare makes it easier to keep in rhythm.

23

Grooves and styles

The rhythms and beats you play depend on the style of music. Here are some examples of styles and the drum grooves they feature.

Rock

Rock music became popular in the 1960s, and it usually features a solid **backbeat** (accenting beats two and four in a 4/4 rhythm). Bands ranging from the Beatles and Rolling Stones through to Oasis, Foo Fighters and Metallica all use a strong backbeat in many of their songs.

Metallica's powerful sound is based around rhythmic rock guitar chords and the solid grooves provided by drummer Lars Ulrich.

Rock pattern

The backbeat is emphasised on beats 2 and 4 in the rock groove shown below.

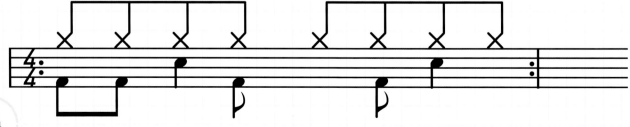

Hip-hop

Hip-hop originated in the Bronx in New York in the early 1970s. The drumbeats are medium in tempo and almost always in 4/4. Hip-hop uses combinations of quarter notes, eighth notes and sixteenth notes to create pulsating grooves.

The DJ Afrika Bambaataa pioneered the development of hip-hop as a new form of popular music.

Hip-hop groove

In this hip-hop rhythm, the groove combines hi-hat, bass drum and snare patterns.

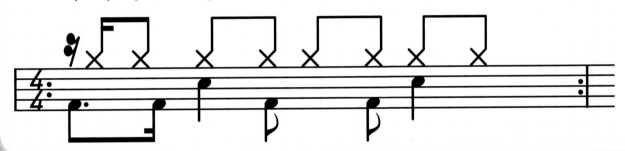

Groove Armada combine dance grooves with guitars, keyboards and vocals.

Dance music

This style contains very repetitive beats and grooves. Originally derived from 1970s' disco music, it usually contains a 'four on the floor' bass-drum pattern (four quarter notes). Daft Punk, Groove Armada, Faithless and Calvin Harris lead the way in this style.

Dance rhythm

This dance pattern features open and closed hi-hats and a quarter-note bass drum groove.

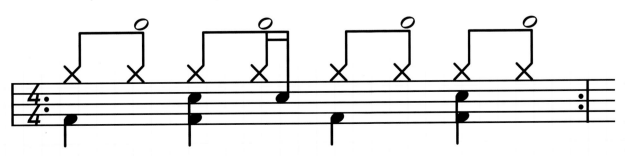

Fascinating rhythms

Here are a few more examples of different musical styles and the rhythms that define them.

R'n'B

Created by African Americans in the late 1940s, R'n'B has now developed into one of the biggest selling musical genres in contemporary music. It is closely related to hip-hop in cultural terms and modern R'n'B incorporates elements of soul, funk and disco in its sound. In the 1970s, bands such as Earth, Wind and Fire helped to develop the style. John Legend, Black Eyed Peas and Beyoncé are some of the biggest names in R'n'B music today.

Earth, Wind and Fire were R'n'B innovators, combining styles to produce new, groove-orientated music.

R'n'B rhythm

R'n'B grooves often feature fast sixteenth-note hi-hats, plus bass drum and snare patterns.

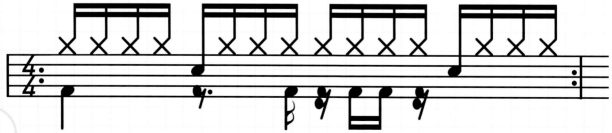

Blues

This style, meaning 'melancholy' feel, was the forerunner to R'n'B, and again was created by African Americans during the early 1900's. Muddy Waters, Stevie Ray Vaughan and John Lee Hooker were all important figures in making this style popular.

Blues guitarist Big Bill Morganfield performs at the Monterey Bay Blues Festival. He is the son of Blues legend Muddy Waters.

12/8 blues shuffle

The middle note of each hi-hat eighth-note triplet is left out, creating a 'shuffling' feel.

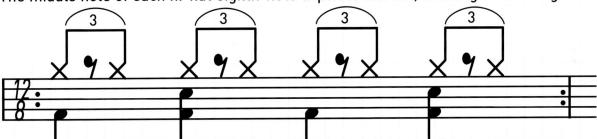

Jazz drummer and composer Donald Edwards.

Jazz

Jazz began in New Orleans around the turn of the 20th century. Many different styles of jazz have developed over the years. In this groove, the ride cymbal gives the pulse and the hi-hat is played with the foot on beats two and four to create a 'jazzy' backbeat.

Jazz groove

The repeating rhythm pattern shown here is a typical jazz groove.

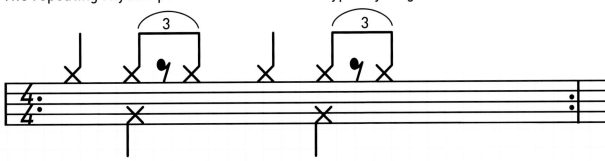

Taking it further

Mastering the drum kit takes a lot of practice. Finding a good music teacher will help, and it is also a great idea to play with other musicians in a band. You can even play along with recordings by your favourite musical artists!

Learning with others

You can find a teacher by going to music shops, by word of mouth, newspaper adverts and the Internet. Going to a music college is an excellent way to further your drum studies. Finding fellow musicians to play with is also a good way to improve your skills and there are many Internet sites designed to put musicians in contact with each other. Your local music shop will also have notice boards for musicians looking for others to play with. It is also great fun to start a band and write your own music.

Top tip

Auditions can be hard work and you should be prepared for rejection. They can also be a fast-track way to becoming a professional musician, increasing your chances of finding yourself the ideal drumming job.

A good drum teacher will teach you correct playing techniques in either one-on-one or group lessons.

Playing live with other musicians will improve your timing – it is the drummer's job to keep everybody locked into a consistent groove.

Musical career

Playing the drums can lead to a career in music, and jobs available to drummers are not limited to playing in a band. You could find yourself teaching the drums or playing on cruise ships, for example. It does not have to stop at playing the drum kit. The skills you will have learnt can be adapted to a wide range of percussion instruments, and mastering these could see you playing in a classical orchestra or a theatre.

Ear training

Try to pick out the drum parts to your favourite songs by listening to them carefully. Start with the hi-hat part, then the snare, the bass drum, and so on. Learn them off by heart – you could even try writing them down. Start with really simple beats until you gain confidence.

Glossary

accent emphasis placed on a particular note that gives it more stress than the others.

acoustic drums drums that make their sound without electronic amplification. They are usually made of wood or synthetic material and have skins pulled tightly across them.

backbeat a consistent rhythm that stresses beats two and four in 4/4 time. In other time signatures, the backbeat will land elsewhere. For example, the backbeat lands on beats four and ten in 12/8 time.

bass lower notes.

brushes special brushes with wire bristles used mostly in traditional jazz drumming to create a quiet rhythm.

crash cymbal a cymbal used to emphasise a certain beat in the song. The sound it makes lasts longer than that of a ride cymbal.

crotchet a type of musical note that usually lasts for one beat in a simple bar of music. Also known as a quarter note.

fulcrum the top joint on the index finger, around which a drumstick should pivot and be held.

metronome a clicking device that sets tempo. It measures time in BPM (beats per minute). A typical mid-range metronome setting for a song would be 120 bpm.

quaver a subdivision of a crotchet beat (a quarter note) into two notes. Also known as an eighth note.

repeat symbols two dots at the start and end of a phrase indicating that the phrase should be played again.

rest a symbol used to indicate that nothing is played for a particular period of time.

rhythm a regularly repeating pattern of beats.

ride (ride cymbal) a cymbal struck with a drumstick to create a steady rhythmic pattern.

sample an electronic recording of a sound or a small piece of music, which can be repeated over and over again.

score in music, the collection of lines and dots indicating what notes are to be played and when.

semibreve a note equal to four crotchets (quarter notes) in 4/4 time. It is also called a whole note.

semiquaver a subdivision of a crotchet (quarter note) into four notes. It is also called a sixteenth note.

solo when a single musician plays part of a piece of music, unaccompanied or with backing from other musicians.

syncopated beat a rhythm that uses dotted notes and where beats that are normally unaccented are accented.

time signature the two numbers, one on top of the other, that appear at the start of a musical score and show how many beats there are in a bar.

Drum and music organisations

There are several organisations aimed at offering advice to drummers, assisting them in finding teachers and helping them to study for examinations.

Rockschool is an organisation set up to provide drum-kit exams and gradings for rock and pop music. It also provides advice to students and teachers.

Trinity Guildhall is an internationally recognised music college that offers drum and percussion exams from beginners to advanced, ranging from Grades 1 to 8.

The Musicians' Union represents professional musicians and also offers advice and guidance for musicians of all ages and abilities.

Further reading

There are plenty of books available for the newcomer as well as the more experienced drummer.

Let's Make Music... On the Drum and Other Percussion Instruments Storey, Rita (Franklin Watts, 2007)

Learn to Play Drums: A Beginner's Guide to Playing Drums Scott, Justin (Apple Press, 2008)

The Drummer's Bible: How to Play Every Drum Style from Afro-Cuban to Zydeco Berry, Mick and Gianni, Jason (Sharp Press, 2004)

Websites

The Internet is a great place to find drumming lessons, information on drumming techniques and advice on how to pursue a career in music.

www.drumming.com
A website containing links to over 5,000 drum lessons, tips, links and articles.

www.virtualdrumming.com
An interactive website featuring virtual drums that you can play in real time, plus online drum lessons and sheet music.

www.rudimentaldrumming.com
Exercises, tips and solos dedicated to building up rudimental drumming skills.

Index